1 & 2. *Beck's Pool* is named after Joseph Beck, one time owner of the *Manor House*. The pool was fed by an overflow from the lake in the grounds of the *Manor House* on the opposite side of Beckspool Road, which was created by Philip Debell Tuckett in 1802. Today *Beck's Pool* is smaller and overlooked by modern houses and flats. A bungalow named *Morpeth Rant* was built by Cecil Fry (of the chocolate family) just behind the tree by the telegraph pole. Both postcards have been used postally, and although dating from the same period, the lower one was posted in 1909 and the upper one in 1964!

3 & 4. This fine double avenue of elm trees ran parallel with Beckspool Road opposite the *Manor House* which can be seen to the right on the upper card. Although the elms have long since been felled, the enormous oysterstone is not far from its position as shown here, as it is now in the front garden of 1 Riverwood Road.

5. The *Manor House* in Beckspool Road was built in 1736 for Joseph Beck in the then fashionable Palladian style. Largely unchanged today, the house is now a home for children with special needs, although the extensive grounds behind the house were developed in the 1960's to form the Manor Estate.

6. *Manor Cottage* actually pre-dates the *Manor House,* but the two properties seem to have belonged together for most of their existence. The building survives today as a residential home and, apart from a small extension on the right, it is largely unchanged when viewed from Beckspool Road.

7. A rear view of *Malmains* in Beckspool Road, which was demolished in the 1930's. It was replaced by a pair of semi-detached houses, *Belsay* and *Ilex House,* and two detached houses - a new *Malmains* and *Ravensdale.* The cellars of the original *Malmains* still exist but are derelict.

Frenchay Lodge. Nr Bristol.   *(J. M. R's School 1897-1899.)*

8. In 1671 the property known as *Frenchay Lodge* next to *Malmains,* was owned by William Woolley. He sold it to Thomas Callowhill whose daughter, Hannah, was married to William Penn, founder of Pennsylvania. The house passed to their son and thus into the Penn family. It was a school from 1897-99, and a childrens' home during the last war. It is now three houses. The central part (the oldest) is called *Penn House.*

FRENCHAY

9. The Friend's Meeting House in Beckspool Road was built between 1670 and 1673, and then rebuilt in 1809. It has always been a place of worship, and amongst those worshipping here were the many Quaker merchants of the village including the Fry family, the Harfords, and the Tucketts. Note the original entrance to *Frenchay Lodge* partly obscured by the horse and trap. This was closed up when *Lodge Cottage* was extended in the 1950's.

10. *Cedar Hall* in Beckspool Road was known as Cedar House until 1862. The oldest part was a farm house (seen on the left) which has been demolished. In the mid 19th century it was a Quaker school for girls. One of the last families to live there was that of Francis MacGregor Fry. The house and estate were developed as flats in the 1960's with only the Georgian façade being retained.

11. Frenchay Parish Hall, known to all as the *Village Hall,* was built by public subscription on land on the corner of Cleeve Road given by Francis Fox Tuckett. Opened in 1909, the architect was Sir George Oatley, better known locally for Bristol's University buildings. The Motosacoche motorcycle has the number Y941, and was owned in 1914 by Walter Hepworth of Horfield, a postcard publisher!

12. A view across the *Common* from Pearces Hill showing *Frenchay Park* on the left, and the fine pair of Georgian houses built by the surgeon Nehemiah Bradford in 1795-99. The righthand house, known as *Bradford's House,* was given as a rectory to the parish in 1840 by Mrs Rooke of *Frenchay Park*, but became a private house again when a new rectory was built in the garden after the last war.

13 & 14. Dating from the middle of the 18th century, *Frenchay Park* and its extensive lands were owned by George Worrall, Lord of the Manor of Winterbourne. He gave the land to build the Parish Church in 1832. In 1916 it was owned by Cosmos Engineering Co., which became the engine division of the Bristol Aeroplane Company. In 1921 it became a children's sanatorium for Bristol, specialising in open air treatments. In 1939-41 it was designated an Air-raid Casualty Hospital (but not used as such), and from 1942-45 it became an American Army Hospital. Apart from losing its fine chimneys, today the house is largely unchanged in its role as the Headquarters of Frenchay NHS Trust.

15. A Post-war aerial view of Frenchay Hospital showing the extensive wards built by the Americans. The hospital was returned to civilian use in August 1945, and has since developed into the major hospital with which we are familiar today. *Frenchay Park,* the original house, is just off the picture on the top right.

16. A post-war picture of what was originally the south lodge of *Frenchay Park*. It is now named *CLIC Cottage* and used for accommodating families of children receiving treatment a long way from home in the hospital. Note the drinking fountain in the middle of the trees on the left of the picture which was erected by Frank and Alice Tuckett to mark Queen Victoria's Diamond Jubilee in June 1897.

FRENCHAY

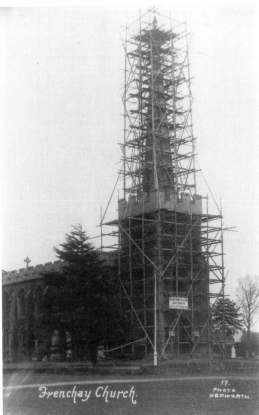

17. In November 1923 the spire of Frenchay Church was badly damaged by lightning and had to be rebuilt. The work can here be seen being undertaken by Alfred Dowling and Son of Bishopston, under the direction of the Diocesan Architect Mr. Hartland Thomas.

18. The Crucifix was erected on the north side of the church by Mrs. Randall Vickers of *Cedar Hall* in memory of the men of the parish who fell in the First World War. It has recently been restored.

19. The interior of Frenchay Church is here pictured with oil lamps before the 1920's. Note the original east window which was damaged during the last war and replaced with clear glass. Before 1900 there was no central aisle as seen here, the pews stretching from side aisle to side aisle.

20. Built during the years 1832-34 the church, dedicated to St. John Baptist, was designed by Henry Rumley and his original drawings still exist. Note the Edwardian dress of those enjoying the timeless pursuit of strolling on the *Common*.

21. The church choir outing to Gough's Caves, Cheddar in 1926. The picture includes Messrs. Attwood, Sharp, Monday, Selkirk, Elliott, Fidler, Criddle, Chamberlain, Mayell, Welshman, Davies and Shepherdson.

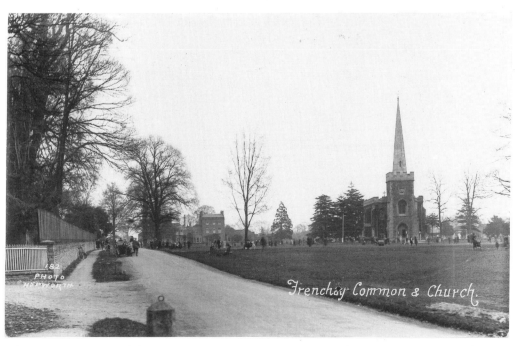

22. A winter scene of the church and *Common* from near the present *CLIC Cottage*.

23. A similar scene in summer, with a cricket match in progress. Frenchay Cricket Club is one of the oldest in the country, and in the 1870's their captain was the famous Dr. W.G. Grace. Unfortunately the club moved from the *Common* in the 1950's, but cricket is still occasionally played on the traditional pitch. The postcard was used postally in 1913.

24. Frenchay School viewed from the south west. The school dates from 1842 when Mrs. Rooks (widow of George Worrall of *Frenchay Park*) gave the land. The two cottages on the right are part of Westbourne Terrace. At one time they were both owned by Frenchay Cricket Club.

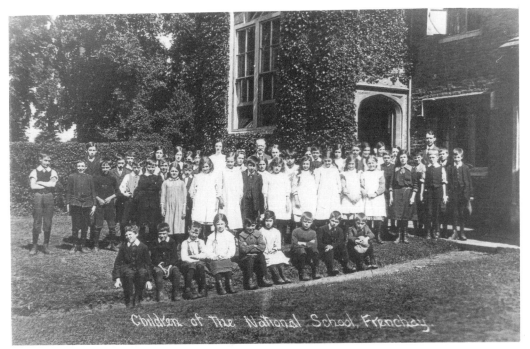

25. The school clad in ivy pictured between 1911 and 1918. The picture includes a teacher, Bessie Whale, and Mr. Wadlow (right rear) who was headmaster from 1894 until 1923. The man standing centre rear was a gardener from one of the big houses, who taught the boys gardening.

26. The school and pupils viewed from the main *Common* at the turn of the century. The centre of the building was the schoolmaster's house, with classrooms on either side – boys on the left – girls and infants on the right. Each classroom was built to hold 89 children!

27. Pupils from the school taking part in a pageant at Christmas 1913. They are (left to right) Beatie Baker, Cecil Palmer, Jack Sharp, Phyllis Hutton, Alec Hutton, Walter Fidler, Molly Guy and Louise Powell – who still lives in Frenchay.

28. Another group from the same pageant. They include Cecil Palmer and Edgar Davey. The other three are unknown.

FRENCHAY

29. A view looking down Frenchay Hill about 1900. The house on the left is *Silver Crag* used in the last century by the Tuckett family as a hospital in times of epidemic. The cottages opposite were replaced by a bungalow about 30 years ago. Today the Post Office is closed and called *Post Office Cottage.* The original Post Office (now called *The Old Post Office)* is across the road, and both were owned by the Vowles and Higgins through two generations.

30. A view up Frenchay Hill from its junction with Quarry Road in the 1950's. *Glenbrook Stores,* the off licence on the right, was run by Mrs. Baber for many years, but is now a private house. Deceptively it is 5 storeys high as it is built up from the floor of the quarry which abuts the road at that point. Beyond is *Silver Crag,* and beyond that the *Old Post Office* of the 1850's.

31. A view up Frenchay Hill from near the bottom. All the cottages in the picture are still there, although the stone surface of the road has given way to tarmac. The lady wearing the white blouse and with her hand on her hip is Alice Chamberlain.

32. The bottom of Frenchay Hill with *Grove Cottage* on the left. The sign above the door reads 'Wm. Whale Boot Maker', and the sign in the garden points to Cleve Tea Gardens opposite. The buildings on the right are the Lower Iron Works, and the sign reads 'T. Moore Frenchay Edge Tool and File Works'. The picture dates from the 1920's.

33. A later post-war picture of the same scene as 32. Established in 1761 the Lower Iron Works was owned at one time by Thomas J. Croome Hobbs, after whom Croomes Hill was named in Downend. The manager's house (since demolished) is the crenellated building. In the near future the whole site is due for re-development.

34. The river side of the Lower Iron Works looking downstream towards Frenchay Bridge. The bridge was built by private subscription in 1788. Despite having a plate on it stating that it is safe for vehicles up to 6 tons in weight, it is now closed to motor traffic.

35. A view from Frenchay Bridge towards the Lower Iron Works. The mill later became a flock mill, making filling for Palliasses for soldiers during the First World War. The Manager's House was at one time a tea garden, and was later called *Fern Cottage*. It spanned the mill stream which can be seen re-joining the river left of the steps.

36. Boating on the Frome upstream of Frenchay Bridge. The cast iron plaque on the face of the bridge reads "Frenchay Bridge built by subscription 1788", and is still there, as is the 'loaf of bread' stone on the parapet.

37. Bullock's Tea Gardens, now *Riverside Cottage,* a private house, at the bottom of Pearces Hill. This was the most notable of the many tea gardens in Frenchay which catered for day trippers in the first half of the century.

38. Frenchay Bridge with the *Thatched Cottage,* a lodge to Oldbury Court Estate, just visible on the left. The wall on the far right of the bridge was the end of Bullock's Tea Gardens.

39. The *Thatched Cottage* viewed from the footpath through Oldbury Court Estate, then called Vassall's after the estate owner. The cottage was occupied for many years early in the century by the Rendals who worked for the Vassall family.

40. The *Thatched Cottage* in its prime in the early years of the century, with the thatch in good repair, and the walls limewashed. It is probable that the man seated in the porch is Mr. Rendal.

41. Even though by the time of this picture the roof had been slated, it was still referred to as *'The Thatched Cottage'!* Unfortunately, the cottage was completely demolished, but the outline of the walls can still be seen in the ground.

42. *Ham's Tea Gardens* was originally a grist mill on Pearces Hill. The small boy is Bertram Ham who was born in 1904. This was one of the first of the many tea gardens in Frenchay in the early part of this century.

FRENCHAY

43. *Ham's Tea Gardens* with Bertram Ham in the foreground with his father standing just behind him. Much of this property has been demolished, but the house remains as a private residence and is called the *Old Mill House*.

44. Frenchay Junior Football Club in April 1920. Pictured left to right are; Back row: E. Ford, F. Guy, Ed. Ford, J. Hobbs, D. Guy. Middle row: Mr. Tucker, W. Hutton, H. Stirling, A. Guy, Mr. C.H.B. Elliott. Front row: L. Stiff, E. Davey, A.F. Hutton, C. Clifford, W. Rawlins.

45. The Frenchay Branch of the Girls Friendly Society in the mid-1930's. The Society was a focus for social activities for young girls away from home working in domestic service in the many big houses in the village. The two ladies seated under the banner are Molly and Nancy Elliott (who started the postcard collection), and second from the right at the rear is May Sawyer who recently gave it to the Frenchay Tuckett Society.

46. Cleve Tea Gardens in Cleevewood Road was formerly Frenchay Upper Iron Works. Before that in 1798 it was a grist mill. The works and cottages are viewed from beside the bridge over the Frome.

47. Cleve Tea Gardens with the path to the right which led to both the tea garden and boats for hire behind the mill. This was the last tea garden in Frenchay to close. It lasted into the 1950's. Now known as *Cleeve Mill* it is a private residence.

48. Taking tea at Cleve Tea Gardens in the early years of the century. The weir is to the right of the picture.

Cleeve Tea Gardens, Frenchay.

49. The rear of the Upper Iron Works with pleasure boaters from Cleve Tea gardens enjoying the river Frome.

Old Mill Wheel, Clevemill Tea Gardens, Downend

50. The water wheel of the Upper Iron Works. The wheel is of the 'undershot' type, and the weir, which is medieval, can be seen on the bottom left of the picture.

51. A rear view of the Upper Iron Works. The mill wheel is in the bottom right corner of this picture, and the weir can be clearly seen.

52. In Cleevewood Road near the bridge was Cleve Wood Pleasure Grounds offering tennis courts and fishing. Adults were admitted for 6d (2½p) and children half price. The picture dates from the early 1920's. The entrance is remarkably unchanged, and now leads to *Cleevewood House* and *Marshfield Park,* both developed as private flats.

53. The front of Clevewood House with Mr. Randall and his family pictured on 25th May 1923. John Randall owned a timber business in Fishponds, and he gave Frenchay Moor to the National Trust just before the Second World War.

54. *Begbrook House* dated from the early 19th century. The house was burnt down in November 1913 by militant suffragettes. The house was unoccupied at the time, and is pictured immediately after the fire as smoke is to be seen rising from the ruins. At one time a bridge over the River Frome connected the property with *Oldbury Court,* Fishponds.

FRENCHAY

55. Another view of *Begbrook House* after the fire. Note the police sergeant standing by the ruins. The house was eventually demolished and a more modest property erected by the Vassall family, but today a modern nursing home also called *Begbrook House* stands on the site which is at the end of Sterncourt Road.

56. Hillside as it descends to the junction of Broom Hill, Frenchay Park Road, and Park Road, looking towards the village of Stapleton. Opposite the lamp in the middle of the road is the entrance to Stoke Park estate, known as Duchess' Gate. The estate became Stoke Park Colony, one of the many hospitals caring for the mentally ill in this area.

STAPLETON

57. The new bridge spanning the river Frome looking up Broom Hill. The wider bridge was built circa 1929, and improvements to the road caused the demolition of *Curtis Mill,* one of many corn mills on the river. The weir still survives, as do most of the buildings seen here.

58. This view shows one of the many mills along the river Frome. They were originally 'grist' or 'corn' mills, later becoming snuff and flock mills. This mill is known as *Snuff Mill,* and was purchased by the City of Bristol for its citizens. Postcard postally used in 1933.

59. This is a view of the park adjoining the *Snuff Mill,* showing the well laid-out flower beds and shrubs, with attractive rustic seats and fencing. Postcard posted in 1935.

60. Looking back to the ruin of *Snuff Mill,* the weir is seen on the left of the mill. Today there is very little of the building left; only the water wheel driving the original mill survives.

61. Another of the mills worked by the power of the river. This one is *Witherlay* or *Parker's Mill,* dating from about 1792. In 1823 it was making snuff for W.D. and H.O. Wills. After falling into decay, it was demolished in the early 1900's. Postally used in 1919.

62. Looking down Colston Hill, an attractive stone stile built into the wall in the foreground. The fields adjoining the lane lead down to the Frome. Higher on the hillside is *Wickham Court,* and further on a cluster of cottages. A delightful view little changed today.

63. Blackberry Hill wending its way past the cottages in Wickham Hill. Beyond are the distinctive buildings of Beaufort Military Hospital as it was known during the First World War. It was used for soldiers recovering from their injuries. The writer of the postcard in 1916 was Private Dixon from Ward 18. His message reads "Progressing favourably, but still in bed. This is a glorious place". Today the buildings are best known as Glenside Hospital.

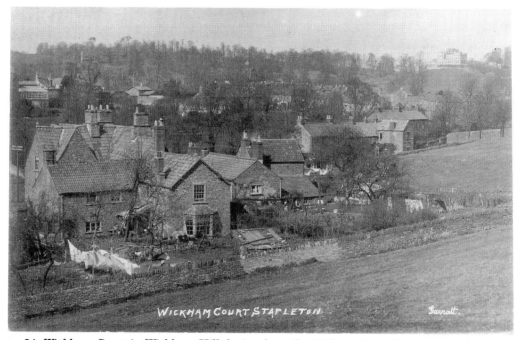

64. *Wickham Court* in Wickham Hill dating from the 16th century. It was in this house that Cromwell and Fairfax met in council of war prior to their successful attack on Bristol. Today the house is largely unchanged.

65. From the grounds of *Stoke Park,* looking towards Purdown with *Heath House* high on the hill. The house and surrounding grounds are much the same today. *Heath House* is now a private psychiatric hospital, the card is by Garratt.

66. *Stoke Park House* from Duchess' Pond, showing its elevated position and extensive grounds. The pond was filled in to build the M32 motorway, but has recently been restored close to its original position.

67. The front of *Stoke Park House*. The house was extensively rebuilt as a fake Jacobean castle by Thomas Wright from designs by Thomas Paty for Norborne Berkeley between 1749 and 1783. The estate passed into the hands of the Beaufort family and was used as a home for the Dowager Duchesses, hence its popular name *"Duchess' House"*. The Beaufort family motto 'Mihi Vobisque' (To me and to you) can be seen above the first floor windows.

68. Duchess' pond, a winter view, the pond surrounded by trees and resident swans. The park keeper patrolling with his gun under his arm, is accompanied by his son and their dog.

69. The same park keeper with his family outside their cottage. Following the Irish troubles in the 1920's, a number of 'Black and Tans' came to the area and were employed by the estate as park keepers.

70. *Frome Lodge* has its entrance in Park Road, and is now divided into flats. This view of the house is from *Wickham Court* across the river. The view is now interrupted by the many trees growing in the valley. The extensive terraced gardens extend down to the river. Used postally in 1930.

71. *Stapleton Court* towards the city end of the village, near Holy Trinity Church. Today it is the Lower School for Colston's Collegiate School, taking boys and girls from the age of 3 up to the age of 11.

72. The Parish Hall in Park Road, an attractive building with an arched doorway, built as a War Memorial to the fallen in the 1914-18 War. The hall is now Stapleton Masonic Hall, and the lettering surrounding the doorway has been removed. The houses on the left are in Brinkworthy Road.

73. Stapleton Post Office in a private house. The post box is in the right hand window of the bay, a telephone box adjoining in the front garden. The owner of the grocery shop next door was G.F. Fursman who also owned a similar shop in Iron Acton. The large house on the other side of Park Road is *Wood Grove*.

74. The staff of the Post Office posing for the photographer in the 1920's. Today the Post office is in a nearby shop, and the house, *Wickham House,* is a private residence, the charming porch still surviving.

75. The fine house on the left is *Wood Grove,* which was demolished in 1933 for road widening. The house on the right jutting out is *Estcourt House* now a residential home, but at one time the home of the Halls who were soap manufacturers. Their products "Easall - the soap Granny used" were made in a small factory below the house. There is a gazebo in the garden which can be reached down the lane.

76. Looking along Park Road towards Frenchay from the grounds of *Holy Trinity Church.* Note the fine iron railings and the lamps on the entrance pillars. This postcard was used postally in 1923.

77. *Holy Trinity,* Stapleton Parish Church, viewed from Bell Hill. This Victorian church was built at his own expense by Bishop Monk who turned nearby Stapleton House (now Colston's Collegiate School) into his palace. Designed by John Norton, the church has a fine commanding west tower and a graceful spire.

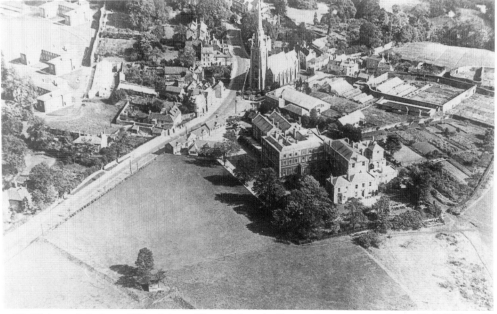

78. This aerial view of Stapleton village taken in the post-war years, shows Bell Hill as it joins with Park Road. The buildings on the left were Stapleton Colony, and the cottage on the extreme left in Bell Hill, *Milton Cottage,* is the birthplace of Frances Trollope the writer, and mother of Anthony Trollope the novelist. The buildings on the right are *Colston's Collegiate School.*

STAPLETON

79. *Holy Trinity Church* and *Colston's Collegiate School* viewed from *Bridge Farm's* fields. The central building of the school is the former Bishop's Palace. Colston's Boys School moved here in 1861 when their former building at the bottom of Colston Street was demolished to build the Colston Hall. The school was founded by Edward Colston in 1708, and the boy poet Thomas Chatterton was a famous pupil.

80. Now in Heath House Lane and known locally as the *Tower Block*, the former folly with its round towers has been converted into private flats known as *Linden House*. Also pictured is *Beech House* once the home of Rajah Ram Mohan Roy, founder of the Hindu Brahma Samaj sect who reject the Caste system. He died here in 1833 and was buried in the grounds. He was re-buried in Arnos Vale Cemetery in 1843, but a stone in the grounds marks his original grave. *Beech House* is also being converted into flats.

81. A view from *Eastville Park* of *Bridge Farm* with two houses, *Sunnybank* and *No.1 Bell Hill,* just visible between the farmhouse and the row of cottages which were used by farm workers. Both these properties were demolished to build the M32 motorway. Between the wars *Bridge Farm* had no fewer than 28 tennis courts and some football pitches on its 200 plus acres. Today only one field is still attached to the farm. Postcard postally used in 1906.

82. A view up Bell Hill with a solid tyred bus making the descent. The cottage behind the bus is a lodge for *Beech House,* since demolished. The boy leading the horse over the bridge towards Wee Lane (known today as Glenfrome Road) is Jack Withers of *Bridge Farm* – he still lives there. The right bank of the river is now occupied by the *Merchants' Arms* public house. Postcard postally used in 1920.

New Bridge & Bell Hill, Stapleton. 756. Bristol.

83. The new bridge over the Frome built to replace the narrow stone bridge in 1929. When the old bridge was demolished a George III guinea was found under its foundation stone. Behind on the left is *Bridge Farm* with *Sunnybank* and the farmworkers' cottages at the bottom of Bell Hill.

On the New Bridge, Bell Hill Stapleton Bristol. 758.

84. This view of the new bridge shows the width of the road which allowed for better traffic flow. The single decker bus heads for the city from Stapleton. The *Merchants' Arms* and the houses in Avery Road are yet to be built.

85. This view of the old bridge looking towards *Eastville Park* and the city. The horse and cart are crossing the bridge in about 1910. The cottage known as the *Old Toll House* dated from 1650, and was in use until 1867 as a Toll House. It was finally pulled down for road widening in 1929.

86. The lower gates of *Eastville Park* bordering Stapleton Road. *Eastville Park* and much of the Frome Valley were purchased for the people of Bristol from Sir Greville Smyth by Bristol City Council following a successful campaign headed by Frank Tuckett of Frenchay in the 1880's.

FRENCHAY INDEX

STAPLETON INDEX